Silvance Onyango Abeka

Corporate customers acceptance of Internet banking

A case study of East African Trade Finance customers

Anchor Academic Publishing

Abeka, Silvance Onyango: Corporate customers acceptance of Internet banking: A case study of East African Trade Finance customers. Hamburg, Diplomica Verlag GmbH 2013

ISBN: 978-3-95489-048-4
Print: Anchor Academic Publishing, an Imprint of Diplomica® Verlag GmbH, Hamburg, 2013

Bibliographical Information of the German National Library:
The German National Library lists this publication in the German National Bibliography. Detailed bibliographic data can be found at: http://dnb.d-nb.de

The digital publication (eBook) of this work with the ISBN 978-3-95489-548-9 can be purchased on the general market or directly from the publisher.

DEDICATION

This work is dedicated to my beloved wife Phoebe and my son Ray for their patience and understanding during the period of my study at Kampala international university.

ACKNOWLEDGEMENT

First of all I give thanks to the almighty God for his mercy and grace granted to me during this time of my degree course and through this research project

I would like to thank my supervisor Prof. Sunday Olwor N. for being there for me whenever I needed him and also offering his professional advice where necessary. I would like also to thank my friends for supporting me in regards to my research.

Am also grateful to my parents, Mr. Jared Abeka and Mrs. Martha Jared, my brothers and sisters, especially Perez for her generous financial and moral support that made me to finish this project successfully and my colleagues staff members of Kampala International University for mounting all the directives, procedures and methods of carrying out this research project.

I would also like to thank the respondents who returned the questionnaires and those who were cooperative to me.

To all those whom i have not mentioned, as well as others whom i have no space to name. I am most sincerely grateful.

May God bless you all.

TABLE OF CONTENTS

CHAPTER ONE

INTRODUCTION

CHAPTER TWO

LITERATURE REVIEW

CHAPTER THREE

METHODOLOGY

CHAPTER FOUR

PRESENTATION AND ANALYSIS OF FINDINGS

APPENDICIES

LIST OF TABLES

LIST FIGURES

ABSTRACT

It is increasingly more interesting to the bank managers to understand what is important to customers when it comes to Internet banking, and especially banking conducted by the customers themselves. Corporate customers and Internet banking has been studied very modestly in the past, and especially the decision-making factors driving customers to go online.

The purpose of this research is to identify the factors that influence corporate customers adoption of Internet banking services in Kenya, Uganda, Tanzania and Rwanda. The hypotheses are empirically evaluated by using Trade Finance customers of an East African bank as the target sample.

Technology Acceptance Model (TAM) is the primary basis for the study. The information gathered from former studies that are mainly concentrating on private customer acts as a foundation for building an extension of TAM suitable for corporate customers.

The study involved 137 respondents from Kenya, Uganda, Tanzania and Rwanda.
Due to the quantitative nature of the study, the results are analysed with statistical measures. This included the use of SPSS to carry out regression analysis. The analysis reveals that corporate users are not motivated by the same factors as private users. In order to become Internet banking customers, it is extremely important for corporate users to have a system that is easy to use and operate with full support from the bank.

CHAPTER ONE

INTRODUCTION

1.0 Introduction

Introduction to the book explains the background and objectives of the study. Also description of the delimitations and structure are included in the first chapter.

1.1. Background of the study

According to Internet World Stats (2000), 5.3 % of the total world population (6,767,805,208) was using the Internet. This means that approximately 360,985,492 people all over the world were connected to each other. Today the situation is very different from that of a couple of years ago. In nine years the amount of Internet users has been increasing by 362.3% (www.internetworldstats.com). These massive figures very well reflect the scope and size of this the network. There is no other channel in the whole world bringing people so close to people, people so close to business or business so close to business than the Internet.

As expected, various industries and business areas are utilizing the Internet. Apart from connectivity, there is a great amount of other prospects coming along with it. The Internet is used to augment, or even supplant, product and service delivery processes considered as more traditional. Banking is not any different from other business areas, as banking in general is extremely information-intensive. Therefore Information technology (IT) has an increasingly important role in modern banking of any kind, especially when directly accessible by the bank's customers.

Originally information technology was utilized in back offices for batch data processing, which was something not that obvious to the customers. Consumer oriented innovations became more important during 1980-1995. This time period is called the "diffusion period of the information revolution in commercial banking" (Bátiz-Lazo and Wood, 2002). Mainly this was possible due to Personal Computers (PC's), which enabled new contacts between banks and customers. But as expected, it didn't end there. After PC's invaded homes and workplaces, customers themselves could start communicating with the bank electronically from their own PC's. The information between customers' PC's and bank's systems did not transfer on-line at that time. Only after emergence of the Internet, banks have been able to provide real-time banking services electronically to a larger audience without a need to install anything on the customer's PC. (Bátiz-Lazo and Wood, 2002)

Not only has the Internet demanded customers to change their habits and even to learn new skills, it has also become a major challenge to banks themselves. The amount and scale of products and services offered online has grown continuously, basically providing something to everyone. Internet has also changed the nature of competition among companies providing banking and investment services. Those having more traditional look on the business are forced to change their view towards the markets. This means taking more proactive approach to providing Internet and mobile services.

Historically branches and physical distribution channels have been the very cornerstones to most banks' market success. However, the emerging electronic channels have forced banks to change their entire management approach. Much of this is thanks to the fact that geographical and time restrictions do not limit the use of banking services anymore (Karjaluoto et al. 2002). As long as customers are connected to the Internet, they should be able to use the services when and where ever. The whole banking strategy has changed as a result of this; people are not dependent on the bank having branch closest to them physically, as it used to be. They can choose whichever bank offering its services online - or even several banks to serve different banking needs. This kind of development has shifted banks' attention more from marketing and selling of services and products towards building and managing customer relations.

According to the research done by Devlin et al. (2003), nearly every bank will have online services available by the year 2011. Surprisingly, they found out that small banks have benefited from the emergence of the Internet: Online services help small banks also to strengthen their competitive position. Internet is contributing to making the competition even fiercer in the future, regardless of the size of the organization (Lüneborg and Nielsen 2003). Internet banking has also played a major role in changing the structure and amount of investments made to develop banking systems. Front-end and back-office systems are now designed to support the online service offerings. Online systems and development of the necessary infrastructure and system architecture receive majority of attention and information technology investments today. Providing real time data, and having the customers to key in the data instead of more experienced bank officers, requires also more from the system design. Although, the investments that have been done also seem to pay off, Lüneborg et al. (2003) discovered that banks providing online services experience a significant positive impact on different performance measures: sales, market share, and amount of new established customer relationships. These are all expected to be profitable at some stage of the lifecycle.

In addition to tangible and measurable benefits brought by online banking, the more intangible ones are no less important, namely competitive advantage, customer retention and attraction. And very promising also for the banks is also that all of the above mentioned benefits eventually result in both increased revenues and reduced costs (Simpson, 2002). On average Internet bank customers are more profitable, maintain larger balances, use more bank products, and are faster in adopting new products and services, especially when compared to customers using more traditional channels (Hitt and Frei, 2002). This may, however, have much to do with the demographics and the background of this type of customers.

Image and reputation of the bank should not be forgotten either: Internet bank offerings have a big influence on the image of the bank, as to the loyalty and satisfaction of the customer (Flavián et al. 2004, Shankar et al. 2002).

It is fairly obvious that bank managers are interested in what can be done to increase the usage of Internet banking services. Understanding customers is important in any service industry. Identifying the elements that influence customers' propensity to start using Internet banking is crucial in the process of acquiring new customers to go online, also it helps with understanding how the customers can be retained. East African banks are not any different in this respect. Nor is the small, traditional area of corporate banking used in this research, called Trade Finance, from other banking areas.

Several studies have been conducted to investigate the issue from private retail customers' point of view in several countries, from several aspects (Sudarraj and Wu 2005, Lassar et al. 2005, Lu et al. 2005, Shih and Fang 2004, Eriksson and Kerem 2004, Akinci et al. 2004, Pikkarainen et al. 2004, Sohail and Shanmugham 2004, Devlin and Yeung 2004, Gerrard and Cunningham 2003, Chau and Lai 2003, Liao and Cheung 2002, Karjaluoto et al. 2002, Suh and Han 2002, Liao et al. 1999, Sathye 1999).

However, what are missing in this stream of research, are those studies looking at the issue from corporate customer's perspective. The only one found was a qualitative study concentrating on the barriers to Internet banking adoption in Taiwan

(Rotchanakitumnuai and Speece, 2002). Trade Finance is a part of corporate banking, and this research aims to find out the factors behind the decisions of corporate customers to start using the Internet services provided by banks In the following sections The researcher discusses the use of Internet and Internet banking in East Africa. In addition he introduces Trade Finance business and products in general level, after which follows an examination of the business area and its role in Internet banking.

1.1.1. Trade Finance

Trade Finance as a phrase is somewhat misleading. To those unfamiliar with this business area, it might sound to be more describing to talk about international trade. Trade Finance involves parties, usually in different countries, importing and exporting goods by using documents as the payment instrument, or using international guarantees to secure that the beneficiary party gets the payment as agreed. When trading partners make a trade agreement, they also have to agree on the payment method used. Trade Finance products are suitable for most of the occasions. These products involve documentary payments, Documentary Credits (D/C) and Collections, and International Bank Guarantees. International Chamber of Commerce (ICC) establishes all rules for Collections, D/Cs and International Bank Guarantees. Those rules are made to be followed by all the parties involved to ensure smooth and reliable trade between all the countries.

1.1.2. Internet banking and Trade Finance

Trade Finance online services can work either two ways, or one way (stand-alone) depending on if the service is connected to the banks systems. Some banks provide online services for all the products, some only documentary payments or different combinations of Trade Finance services.

When talking about online Trade Finance services, two way online services mean that the communication is done interactively: providing the customer a way of taking care of their Trade Finance business electronically via the Internet, sending and receiving transactions to and from the bank. Customers can make applications electronically, meaning they can issue deals (Import D/C's, Export Collections and Outgoing Bank Guarantees) to the bank, and receive issuances of deals (Export D/C's, Import Collections and Incoming Bank Guarantees) electronically from the bank. In addition to that, they can make amendments to the deals registered in the system, receive notifications and correspondence with the bank electronically, accept documents and payments and follow the status of their deals.

Stand-alone service refers to a service that is not connected to the banks systems in any way. It merely offers the customer an electronic way of filling in applications and saving historical data on the deals.

Online services usually provide the customer also a way of collecting historical data, making reports of them and using the deal information in various ways. For example the data saved is used to support accounting and bookkeeping for controlling and following up the company cash flow, liabilities and transactions.

The aim of this study is to distinguish the factors influencing corporate customers' when they make a decision to start using Internet banking services or not. The empirical evaluation is based on Trade Finance customers and their view on a specific Internet banking service provided.

1.2 Statement of the problem

Corporate customers have several factors that influence them to adopt internet banking when transacting their financial business. Banks need to understand which factors may influence and attract customers to use internet banking, so that they can build long relationships with existing customers. Trust has been seen as a key factor in successful relationship marketing (Morgan and Hunt, 1994). Building a long relationship with customers can be the most important requirement for international and local banks so that they can keep their position in the market and compete globally. Banks should understand how they can attract customers from different countries, cultures, and backgrounds to use their services both online and offline. Factors that influence corporate customers' decision to adopt internet banking should be instigated.

In order to understand how banks can maintain good or successful relationship with customers and attract them to use internet services, Commitment-Trust Theory (Morgan and Hunt, 1994) and the Technology Acceptance Model (Davis et al., 1989) can be used as a basic for this study.

1.3 Purpose of the study

The purpose of this quantitative study was to identify the factors that influence East African corporate customers' adoption of online banking services.

1.4 Objectives of the project

There are two levels of objectives the researcher considered such as main and specific objectives.

1.4.1 General objectives

The major objective of this quantitative study was to identify the factors that influence East African corporate customers' adoption of online banking services. The first step was to investigate the background of previous research done on the area, especially Technology Acceptance Model, as it was used as the basis for the theoretical framework of this study. The conclusion of the theory was done based on discussions with Trade Finance specialists of the Kenya Commercial bank (referred to as the case bank in the remainder of the study). The theoretical model and hypotheses constructed to test it, was an extension to the Technology Acceptance Model.

1.4.2 Specific objectives

i. To find out how technology factors can mediate the effects of trust on corporate customers' intentions to use internet banking by East African Trade Finance.

ii. To find out if perceived ease of use of internet affect customers' decisions at East African Trade Finance.

iii. To discover which of the technological factors can best mediate the effect of the trust's antecedents on customers' intentions to use internet banking at East African Trade Finance.

iv. To find out if Bank Support can influence corporate customers to adopt internet banking across East Africa.

1.5 Research Questions

i. How does technology factors mediate the effects of trust on corporate customers' intentions to use internet banking by East African Trade Finance?

ii. Does perceived ease of use of internet affect customers' decisions at East African Trade Finance?

iii. Which of the technological factors can best mediate the effect of the trust's antecedents on customers' intentions to use internet banking at East African Trade Finance?

iv. Does Bank Support influence corporate customers to adopt internet banking across East Africa?

1.6 Research Hypotheses

i. Perceived Usefulness positively influences use of Trade Finance Internet Services in East Africa.

ii. Perceived Ease of Use positively influences use of Trade Finance Internet Services in East Africa.

iii. Organizational Support positively influences use of Trade Finance Internet Services in East Africa.

iv. Bank Support positively influences use of Trade Finance Internet Services in East Africa.

1.7 Scope

As a background of the study the researcher used mainly Technology Acceptance Model related research that in general examine user acceptance of online banking solutions. Although these studies cover wide variety of countries and aspects to the topic, most of them are related to retail banking. This research was about Trade Finance services offered to corporate customers in the Internet by one bank, within East Africa. Despite the case study nature of the research, the believe the results of this research were generalized to other Internet services designed for corporate customers, and especially for Trade Finance. Despite the fact that geographical limitations of this research narrowed down the amount of countries involved to four, generalization of the results can be done also in other so called African countries with society similar to the East

Africa. The research data was collected, analyzed and presented over the course of six month period.

1.8 Significance Of The Study

The primary benefit of this study is as a contribution to knowledge in the areas of Internet banking adoption and factors that influence its adoption. The research will contributes to the limited number of empirical researches on internet banking.

This research did an assesment on the current use of internet in banking sector in East Afica, hence try to provide some improvement recommendation on internet banking adoption there. This paper also highlight the potential power of internet banking as the main tool to promote rapid growth and expansion of banks with the simple and convenient facilities guided by internet.

The study also provide great benefits for researchers, and educators though providing a clearer view and deep understanding for all the issues related to the field of Electronic Banking. The university and its authorized personel are permissible to use this paper for academic reference. The study will also act as a valuable resource for reference in literature review for those intending to do further research on e- banking related topics and finally, It will contribute value and input to the pull of the already existing knowledge by confirming theories that exist and making recommendation to the new facts.

The study can also be a guide the e- banking institutions and other policy makers use to put strong policies that will help the entire economy if at all adoption of internet banking has challenges it is bringing to the economy as well as the customers and other stakeholders.

This paper provide the Information System practitioners with more insight on strategic determinants of adoption of internet banking thereby making their work of conducting research, planning, developing and improving computer based information systems, software and related concepts, developing principles and operational methods as well as to maintaining information systems easier by ensuring integrity and security of data.

Today there is an on-going debate and criticism of internet money transfer services, often originating from the banking industry. In many countries there is yet to be a clear statement whether or not the new services interferes with traditional banking, and if the same regulatory principles should be required for transfer services as for banking services. The heavy regulations of the banks have previously not been imposed on transaction based services. The data and analysis of this project is not only valuable for other countries that is in the making of implementing similar services (and many are), but also to regulators of the technology and any organization or company that wants to utilize a new infrastructure to distribute and transfer money. This could be local entrepreneurs, developers of the services or aid organizations to name a few examples. In order to design better financial services one must look at the needs and behavior of the users. In which direction are these services heading? If a new way of banking is formed that is evolving from transactions instead of savings, will it differ from what we have today? Much can be learnt from the successful implementations of these services in Scandinavia, also for services based in the developed world.

1.9 Conceptual frame work.

The framework proposed that customers' loyalty can be influenced by customers' intentions to use internet banking. It also proposed that customers' intentions to use internet banking can be affected by customers' attitudes toward using internet banking. When customers have positive attitudes, they are more likely to adopt internet banking and vice versa.

The framework hypothesized that customer' attitudes toward internet banking can be affected by both perceived usefulness and ease of use. Customers' perceived usefulness can be determined by perceived ease of use, customers' self-efficacy, and customers' trust, while their perceived ease of use can be affected by customers' trust and customers' self-efficacy to use internet in general and online banking in particular.

The framework proposed that customers' self-efficacy can be delivered by their technological experiences. Finally, it suggested that customers' trust can be determined by shared value including security system and customers' privacy, banks/customers communication, banks' reputation in markets, Organization Support, Banks' Support and customers experiences. All these factors will influence corporate acceptance of internet banking within East African Trade finance.

The following was the proposed framework which shows the casual relationships between factors addressed:

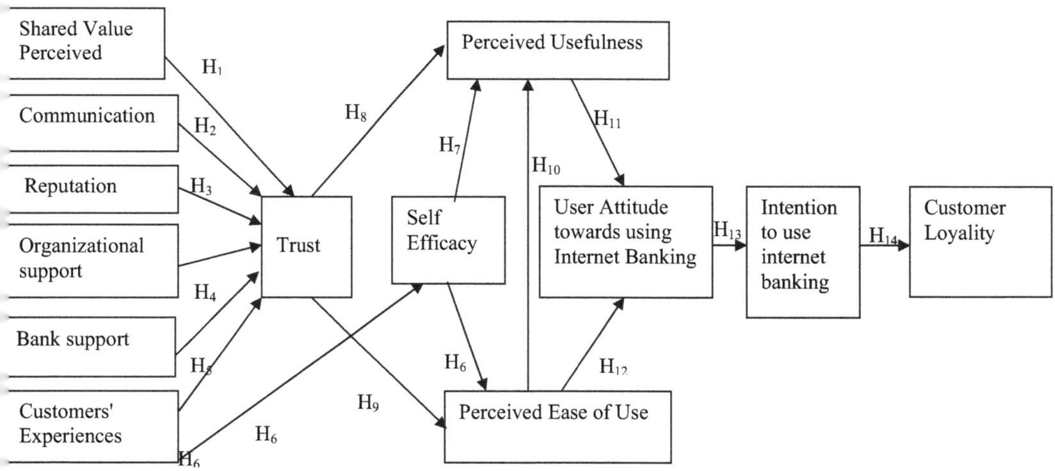

Figure 1.1. Study Frame work

Source: (Researcher,2009)

CHAPTER TWO

LITERATURE REVIEW

2.0 Introduction

In this chapter I present the research that has been done in the area of user acceptance of technology in the context of Internet banking, as well as adoption of Internet banking. First there is a brief overview of the field in general. After that I discuss about the relevant empirical studies done about Technology Acceptance Model and Internet banking, as well as other research about adoption of Internet banking. To complete the theoretical background, studies using Technology Acceptance Model with other information systems are included. As a summary of the reviewed literature, state of the art of the research this far is analysed. Finally I discuss the major findings relevant to this study, and research limitations necessary to take into consideration.

2.1 Overview of the field

User acceptance of technology has been studied repeatedly over the decades from various perspectives. The more important technology becomes as a part of our daily lives, the more companies expect their customers, suppliers and employees to be willing and able to utilize technology in various ways. It is understandable that at the same time research done in and around this subject has become more and more important. Several models describing and predicting the reasons for users accepting or rejecting a piece of technology have been created and evolved during the years.

However, most of them are very much alike, and based on same pioneering findings made decades ago.

Theory of Reasoned Action (TRA), Theory of Planned Behavior (TPB) and Technology Acceptance Model (TAM) are probably the most used theories for modelling user adoption of new technology. TRA and TPB are mostly used in the studies of social psychology to study the behaviour of people. Researchers of system usage and information technology adoption have also extensively adopted them. TRA is in fact the ancestor of both TPB and TAM.

Technology Acceptance Model is an information systems theory, which is adapted from TRA. It is widely used for the purpose of predicting, explaining and enhancing common understanding of user acceptance of information technology in various areas. This research uses the findings based on TAM as the basis for the theoretical model: Also because TAM has been used in many similar studies earlier. Several extensions of TAM have been proposed and empirically validated also in studies conducted in the area of Internet banking – especially on the retail side of it. Overall, Internet banking, e-commerce and other information technology and information system adoption have been increasingly popular topics among researchers. This has been the trend over the last decade. In addition to Technology Acceptance Model, other theoretical approaches have been used to increase general understanding. As mentioned before, the theories remind very much each other. Regardless of the theory used, the researches support each other in terms of factors and determinants identified.

Technology Acceptance model is introduced in more detail in the following sections in order to explain the foundation for this research.

2.2 Technology Acceptance Model

Technology Acceptance Model (TAM) was initially suggested by Fred Davis in 1989. It is one of the most studied and used models in the investigations of user acceptance of information technology. The model is adapted from Theory of Reasoned Action (TRA), which was originally proposed by Fishbein and Ajzen in 1975. Technology Acceptance Model is an information system theory, which purpose is simply to predict and explain the user acceptance of information technology. The model addresses the reasons why users either accept or reject particular piece of information technology. The revised model by Davis et al. (1989) is constructed from external variables (external stimulus), perceived usefulness and perceived ease of use (cognitive response), behavioral intention, and actual usage (behaviour). (Davis et al. 1996a)

2.3 Original Technology Acceptance Model

This figure is a description of the original TAM by Davis.

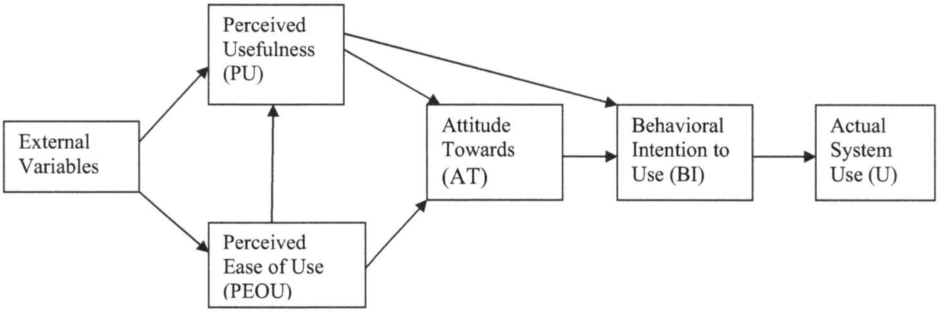

Source:- (Davis, 1989)

Figure 2.1 Original Technology Acceptance Model

The fundamental idea of the theory is that perceived usefulness and perceived ease of use influence the users' intention to use information technology either directly or mediating via attitude towards the behaviour, leading to actual usage of the system. Attitude Towards (AT) and Behavioural Intention (BI) are common with the Theory of Reasoned Action. Perceived ease of use (PEOU) has a strong influence on AT through perceived usefulness, but also directly. Perceived Usefulness (PU) has a strong direct influence via both AT and BI.

PU was defined as "the degree to which a person believes that using a particular system would enhance his or hers job performance". "A system high in perceived usefulness, in turn, is one for which a user believes in the existence of a positive use-performance relationship". PEOU was described as "the degree to which a person believes that using a particular system would be free from effort". (Davis, 1989). The original TAM was revised by leaving attitude from the model, as empirical validation proved that intention to use is only partly mediated by attitude (Davis and Venkatesh. 1996a).

2.4 Revised Technology Acceptance Model

This figure is a description of the revised TAM by Davis and Venkatesh.

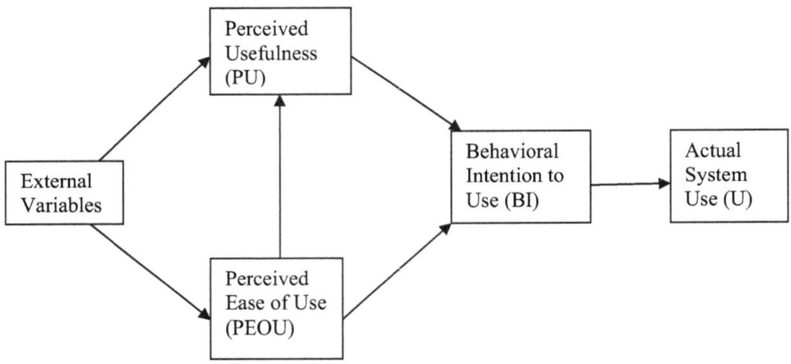

External Stimulus **Cognitive Response** **Intention** **Behavior**

Source:- (Dav s and Venkatesh, 1996)

Figure 2.2 Revised Technology Acceptance Model

Although TAM has been found to be very good in explaining user acceptance of technology, it has been further developed. In 2000, Davis and Venkatesh extended the theory and created TAM2. "TAM2 incorporates additional theoretical constructs spanning social influence processes (subjective norm, voluntariness, and image) and cognitive instrumental processes (job relevance, output quality, result demonstrability, and perceived ease of use)." (Davis et al, 1989). Furthermore Venkatesh et al. (1996) created a unified model called Unified Theory of Acceptance and Use of Technology (UTAUT). They compared eight models, developed and empirically validated UTAUT, which proved to outperform all the existing models from the past.

Szajna (1996) empirically tested TAM by measuring both self-reported and actual usage in pre- and post-implementation. She found the model to be successful in predicting both. Legris et al. (2003) critically reviewed TAM by using 22 articles from 1980 to 2001. The articles were empirical studies using TAM respecting its integrity. Only few studies used all of the original variables, mainly they left out AT, which is in coherence with the revised TAM.

The limitations of the reviewed researches were related to frequent use of students as the empirical sample, examining office automation software or systems development applications, and self-reported usage. The conclusion of the critical review was that TAM is a useful theoretical model, but it should be integrated to a model including variables from human and social change processes, as well as innovation adoption model. TAM explains normally about 40 percent of the variance in intention to use and usage behaviour, which further supports the perception of TAM's suitability in this type of research (Legris et al 2003, Pikkarainen et al. 2004).

2.5 Technology Acceptance Model and Internet banking

Quite a few researchers have applied TAM when studying acceptance of Internet banking. Liao et al. (2002) even made an invariance analysis concluding that TAM is a well suitable instrument for evaluating Internet banking acceptance, but also that the suitability is independent of the respondent characteristics such as gender, age and information technology competence. The current research done about Internet banking and Technology Acceptance Model are reviewed next, presenting the major findings of them and the empirical environment.

Sudarraj et al. (2005) used deconstructed TAM to measure the importance of usefulness and ease of use in online and telephone banking. They successfully validated the model with Canadian university students. Karjaluoto et al. (2002) built a model based on TRA and TAM, which was empirically tested with private Finnish retail bank customers. Their conclusion is, that "prior computer experience, prior technology experience, personal banking experience, reference group, and computer attitudes strongly affect attitude and behaviour towards online banking." (Karjaluoto et al. 2002).

Supporting findings were those of Lassar et al. (2005) who studied online banking adoption in the United States in the light of TAM. They concluded that the intensity of Internet usage is significantly influencing individuals' adoption of Internet banking. These findings suggest that the more experienced the consumers are in using the computers and the Internet, the more likely it is that they will start using Internet banking.

Another Finnish study investigated consumers' acceptance of online banking: Pikkarainen et al. (2004) added perceived enjoyment, information on online banking, security and privacy and quality of Internet connection to the model. Surprisingly, they found only PU and information of online banking significantly affecting use of Internet banking services in Finland. Hong Kong students were used to empirically test another modification of TAM; in this study Chau and Lai (2004) also discovered that PU could be the only major factor directly influencing the attitude towards online banking. PEOU influenced also directly, but mainly via PU. Other measured factors like alliance services, personalization and task familiarity influenced through PU, and accessibility through PEOU.

Suh and Han (2002) added trust to the original TAM model. They studied their model by empirically evaluating responses from personal customers of five major banks in South Korea and discovered trust to be a very significant determinant of user acceptance of Internet banking. Eriksson et al. (2004) made the same conclusion while studying the meaning of trust with Estonian private customers. Trust had a significant positive effect on both PEOU and PU, out of which PU appeared to be stronger in predicting the intention to use Internet banking.

Trust was handled also by Wang et al. (2003). Their research aimed on recognizing the determinants of user acceptance of Internet banking. In this research they introduced perceived credibility as a new factor to TAM, in addition to self-efficacy, perceived usefulness and perceived ease of use. The model was empirically tested by phone interviews
with Taiwanese consumers. Surprising results were found: perceived ease of use and perceived credibility were more significant than perceived usefulness in predicting the behavioural intention to use Internet banking. The surprising factor in this was, that majority of TAM related research has concluded that PU is the ruling factor over PEOU. Self-efficacy again was found to have significant effect through the three abovementioned factors.

2.6 Adoption of Internet banking

Factors familiar from TAM have been used in studies based on other theories and theoretical frameworks. The research methods and results resemble each other very much. Liao and Cheung (2002) empirically measured perceived usefulness and its attributes with retail customers in Singapore. They found out that "individual expectations regarding accuracy, security, transactions speed, user friendliness, user involvement, and convenience were the most important quality attributes in the perceived usefulness of Internet based e-retail banking".

Supporting some of the findings in Singapore, ease of use, Internet accessibility, awareness, trust and security concerns, convenience and attitude towards change were identified as main factors that affect the adoption of Internet bank services in Malaysia (Sohail and Shanmugham, 2003). Rotchanakitumnuai and Speece (2003) made a qualitative research among Thai corporate customers, which revealed that for corporations trust and security concerns were major barriers together with lack of organizational support (lack of IT resources, knowledge, management support, and training).

Akinci et al. 2004 compared users and non-users in the process of trying to identify the factors influencing adoption among sophisticated consumer segments in Turkey. They stated that non-users were not aware of all the benefits of Internet banking and did not believe in receiving adequate help for problem solving when using Internet services. The non-users preferred traditional channels because of lacking in confidence in using Internet banking and worrying about making incorrect transactions, where as the users believed quite the opposite. These problems were identified already by Sathye (1999) in Australia almost 10 years ago: difficulty in use, resistance to change, lack of awareness, and benefits of Internet banking were standing out as the obstacles for beginning to use the online services. The research results suggest that the problem of difficulty to use could be addresses by banks giving better education to the customer. According to Sathye (1999), Customers also expect the banks to give comprehensive information on the benefits before adopting the service.

2.7. Research on Technology Acceptance Model in other context than Internet banking

Igbaria and Iivari (1995) extended Technology Acceptance Model in research about the effect of self-efficacy on computer usage in Finnish companies. Their TAM incorporates self-efficacy and the determinants of it (experience and organizational support) as the factors having an impact on computer anxiety, perceived ease of use and perceived usefulness and finally the actual use of computer technology. Self efficacy, computer experience and organizational support were proven to have significant direct effect on perceived ease of use. The results imply that "perceived ease of use plays very important role in mediating the relationships between experience, anxiety and self-efficacy and perceived usefulness." Furthermore, "self efficacy, computer anxiety, perceived ease of use and usefulness partially mediate the effect of experience and organizational support on self-reported usage behaviour" (Igbaria and Iivari, 1995).

In line with the findings of the studies in Internet banking, Igbaria and Iivari, also stated that perceived usefulness had the biggest direct effect on actual system usage. Davis and Venkatesh (1996b) then again modelled the antecedents of perceived ease of use, concluding that one of the most important variables influencing perceived ease of use was self-efficacy.

Deriving from Iivari and others, McFarland and Hamilton (2004) studied computer anxiety, system quality, prior experience, others' use, organizational support and task structure and their influence on computer-efficacy, perceived usefulness, and perceived ease of use and system usage. They discovered that system usage is significantly influenced by all of the abovementioned factors. They empirically tested the model with answers from users in US companies.

Yi and Hwang (2003) again studied self-efficacy, enjoyment, and learning goal orientation also in the context of TAM with university students. They used web-based class management system as the piece of technology examined. Self-efficacy appeared to directly influence the use, whereas enjoyment and learning goal orientation mediated through self-efficacy, usefulness and ease of use. Usefulness and ease of use in turn influenced the decision to use through behavioural intention.

There are many similarities between adopting other e-commerce activities and Internet banking. In many ways the reasons for adoption or rejection are alike. Eastin (2002) examined four different e-commerce activities (shopping, banking, investing and online services) and their diffusion in the United States. The outcome was that selfefficacy, amount of internet use, perceived convenience, perceived economic advantage, and overall adoption of similar innovation positively have positive influence to the overall adoption of e-commerce. According to them, perceived risk has a negative impact, and therefore it works as a barrier to adoption of any kind of ecommerce.

Jiang et al. (2000) utilized TAM in their empirical study about user behaviour and ecommerce. Their model had five constructs: utilization of the Internet, near term consequences, facilitating conditions and experience with the Internet. They found out that the most important driving factor influencing the utilization of the Internet is prior experience. Another significant positive relationship was found between facilitating conditions and utilization of the Internet. This implies that the more familiar the users are with the Internet, and the better they feel they can get information from the sites, the more likely they are to use the Internet service in question.

2.8 Analyses of the state of the art

As already mentioned before, Technology Acceptance Model is widely and successfully used in the research about adoption of Internet banking. The model has been criticized for being almost too easy to generalize to any piece of information technology. However, it can also be the strength of it, as it is fairly easy to extend the model with other theories and models. This can be seen from the amount of research in the Internet banking area. The resemblance of studies not utilizing TAM and those that are, can be easily seen. Same factors, variables and determinants are empirically tested with slightly different sample and method.

The validity and reliability of the studies is good, although many of the studies are using university students as the sample. The use of such homogenized data can lead to results that are not applicable to the entire population of the respective country, for example. On the other hand the variety of countries and continents studied is satisfying for generalizing the research outcomes, also keeping in mind that the results are similar also in those studies that are using data with more invariance. Europe, North America, Asia, Australia, and Baltic countries, developing and developed countries have been covered with results supporting each other. Thus, the research items can be used to support the building of the model for Trade Finance banking in Scandinavian countries.

2.9 Summary

Technology Acceptance Model was chosen as a basis for this study. The reason for choosing it is that the model has been successfully used in several previous researches related to retail bank customers. Additionally, similar determinants can be acknowledged to influence the user acceptance and adoption of Internet banking, whether or not these studies have been using Technology Acceptance Model as the framework. The following seven items have been identified as common determinants of predicting the adoption of Internet banking and other type of e-commerce or information systems, and therefore selected for closer investigation in this research:

- **Perceived Usefulness** "The degree to which a person believes that using a particular system would enhance his or hers job performance" (Davis,1989)

- **Perceived Ease of Use** "The degree to which a person believes that using a particular system would be free from effort". (Davis, 1989)

- **Self Efficacy** A person's estimate of his/her ability to cope with using a particular system.

- **Previous Experience** Prior experience with similar technology.

- **Organizational Support** The importance of support the customer receives From his own organization.

- **Bank Support** The importance of support the customer receives From the vendor, in this case a bank.

- **Awareness** The level of awareness about the particular system And using it.

The reviewed literature works as a good basis in developing a model to measure the factors that influence East African corporate customers and their decision on whether or not to use the bank's Internet services.

The following chapter introduces the model, which includes presenting the chosen factors and their occurrence in the previous literature, as well as construction of the hypotheses to be tested in order to validate the model.

CHAPTER THREE

METHODOLOGY

3.0 Overview

This chapter provides a detailed description of the research methods that was used in the study in order to accomplish the research objectives. It gives the plan, structure and strategies that were used to prove the research hypotheses. The chapter covers the research design, research population, sampling procedure, research instruments, research procedure, Data analysis, Ethical considerations and limitations of the study.

3.1 Research Design

This study adopted basically correlation and survey research design. This study led to establish the factors that influence corporate customers to adopt online banking. The researcher was interested in this study due to constant inconveniencies that the corporate customers get when they need to transact banking business at odd hours when the banks are closed, it also enables the organization to run smoothly and deliver to the society. The clients' data will be safe and will not risk losing their money and will boost the clients' confidence in the company and the company will grow. The researcher collected data from business process in the organization, Corporate Customers, Current system if any,. The researcher used questionnaires and observation guide to collect the data, which he processed through dating, coding and classification.

3.2 Research population

The researcher targeted population was business process in the organization, corporate Customers, Current system if any, Capability of the organization's technology infrastructure and the management of the organization. The study involved a total of 472 customers from Kenya, Uganda, Tanzania and Rwanda.

3.3 Research Instruments

Quantitative analysis was chosen to test the research model, as it is good for measuring how many and in what proportion. In addition, with statistically reliable quantitative research it is possible to generalize the results: if the same questions are asked from different people with the same characteristics, the answers should support the outcome of the study.

The method for collecting empirical data for the statistical analysis was customer survey. Questionnaires were sent out to randomly selected Trade Finance customers of the case bank; (Kenya Commercial Bank) in Kenya, Uganda, Rwanda and Tanzania. The questionnaires were developed together with this banks best Trade Finance specialists. With the help of the expertise of these specialists, the questionnaire content and validity of the questions were confirmed to facilitate achieving the goal of the study in the best possible way. In addition the questionnaires contained questions outside of this research, mainly related to customer service and open-ended comments. The responses to those questions are used for further analysis only for the case bank's purposes.

The questionnaire was divided into 3 parts: Part 1 handled demographics and data related to user background and usage of the system in general. In part 2 the Likert 5 scale closed end questions were included for testing the hypothesis. Part 3 contained open questions for the customers to express their thoughts with free text.

The Likert 5 scaling selected for this research is a one-dimensional scaling method. This scale was chosen because it has been widely used in previous researches, and is often used for testing hypothesis, or scoring records. Both of those methods are used in analysing the results. Therefore the researcher decided to use Likert scale from 1 to 5 for the questions in part 2 designed for hypothesis testing. The following scale was applied in the survey:

1. = totally disagree
2. = disagree
3. = undecided
4. = agree
5. = totally agree

The questionnaire was translated from English (appendix A) to Kiswahili language which is dominant within East Africa region. Informative cover letters written in Kiswahili was also included in the mails with pre-paid return envelopes. Some copies of the questionnaires were sent to all customers by mail at the beginning of November in

2009. The responses were then received by mail during the following 3-4 weeks in late December and beginning of January 2010.

Before going to the field the researcher obtained an introduction letter from office of the Director of School of Post Graduate. This introduced the researcher as a student attempting to carry out an academic research.

The researcher visited libraries and searched for data related to the study. The data collected was then sorted and categorized after which it was analyzed. The conclusions and recommendations then made.

The survey questions and their relation to the hypotheses are presented in the table below.

Table 3.1. Questionnaire questions for hypothesis testing

FACTOR	VARIABLE	HYPOTHESIS	SURVEY QUESTION
Perceived usefulness	PU	H1	I find / I think I would find TFIS useful in conducting Trade Finance banking transactions
Perceived ease of use	PEOU_1	H2	a) I find / I think I would find it easy to do what I want to in TFIS
	PEOU_2	H2	b) I find / I think I would find TFIS easy to use
Organizational support	OSU_1	H3	a) It is / would be important for me to have someone else in my organization to help out in case of non-technical* problems with TFIS
	OSU_2	H3	b) It is / would be important for me to have someone else in my organization to help out in case of technical** problems with TFIS
Bank support	BSU_1	H4	a) It is / would be important for me to have someone to help out in the bank in case of nontechnical* problems with TFIS
	BSU_2	H4	b) It is / would be important for me to have someone to help out in the bank in case of technical** problems with TFIS

* Non-Technical problem could be for example creating a template, finding a deal via Inquiry, etc)

**Technical problem could be for example getting an error message or being logged out in the middle of a transaction

3.4 Ethical considerations

The study was primarily engaged in all sorts of target corporate customers who where viewed necessary for data collection and some selected key informants. Accordingly during the course of the study, the researcher provided personal or commercially valuable information about himself to the respondents. Then before an individual become a respondent of the study, he/she was notified of the aims, methods, anticipated benefits and the hazards of this study. Secondly it was a respondent's right to abstain from participation in this study and his/her right to terminate at any time. The confidential nature of their replies was promised and no pressure or inducement of any kind was applied to encourage an individual to become a respondent of the study.

3.5. Data Analysis Method

The analysis was done with a system designed for statistical analyses (SPSS). Descriptive statistics and regression analysis, completed with Pearson product-moment correlation analysis, were selected as the methods for interpreting and analysing the empirical data. With the help of these statistical measures, the validity of the theoretical model and hypothesis are tested.

Regression analysis was chosen, for it fits well for hypotheses testing and analysing how independent variables can be used to predict a dependent variable. Linear regression is based on correlation between the variables, in this case Pearson product-moment correlation, but it enables more detailed and sophisticated examination of the interrelationship of the variables. As David Stockburger says:

> *"Regression models are powerful tools for predicting a score based on some other score. They involve a linear transformation of the predictor variable into the predicted variable. The parameters of the linear transformation are selected such that the least squares criterion is met, resulting in an "optimal" model. The model can then be used in the future to predict either exact scores, called point estimates, or intervals of scores, called interval estimates"* (Stockburger, 1998)

Fitness of the model built for this study is examined by this kind of standard regression analysis. The analysis shows how much of the total variance in the dependent variable (use of the system) is possible to explain by the independent variables; perceived usefulness, perceived ease of use, self-efficacy, previous experience, awareness, organisational support, and banks support.(Pallant, 2001)

Analysis called ANOVA is conducted in order to determine the statistical significance of the correlations between the selected variables. The p-value of the F-test indicates the level of association between the dependent and independent variables in the model. When the significance p-value is less than 0.05, it means there is a statistically significant association between the dependent and independent variables. P-value 0.10 refers to weakly significant association. If the p-value is more than 0.10, then the model chosen is not statistically significant.

The Pearson product-moment correlation was added to conclude the regression analysis. The idea for the use of this correlation measure is to find out how much the dependent variables selected (PEOU_1, PEOU_2, SEF, OSU_1, OSU_2, BSU_1 and BSU_2) correlate with actual use of the system, and what are their relationships. Also the regression analysis correlations are based on Pearson product-moment correlation. In addition to the automatic 2-tailed significance indicator selected for the analysis, the rules for determining the strength of the relationship applied are as presented in table 3.2:

Table 3.2. Strength of relationship based on Pearson correlation

Pearson correlation	Relationship
0.10 to 0.29 or -0.10 to -0.29	Small
0.30 to 0.49 or -0.30 to -0.49	Medium
0.50 to 1.0 or -0.50 to -1.0	Large

Note, that the negative sign is only referring to the direction of the relationship, not the strength of the relationship. (Pallant, 2001 ref. Cohen, 1988)

3.6. Validity, reliability, generalizability

The sample companies chosen were randomly selected, and due to this randomness they represent various company sizes and industries. Therefore the results can be generalized to reflect the East African companies doing export and import. Although the customers were selected among Kenyan, Ugandan, Tanzanian and Rwandan Trade finance customers of the case bank, they can and do use the services also from other banks, which was obvious from couple of the answers. It is somewhat common that the customers have some part of their business in another bank, and other set of services from another bank. One of the reasons why it is very important for the bank managers to understand how the customers think to be able to compete in the best possible way.

Although the questionnaires in each country were sent out in local language, they were all based on the English questionnaire, and therefore fundamentally the same. This applies also to the cover letters that were attached to the questionnaire, explaining to the customers the nature of the research and its purpose. Thus, all the respondents received the same questionnaire with same data content, in the same format via post mail.

Both males and females are represented, though majority of the responses were received from females. It is highly likely that this reflects the division of gender among personnel taking care of import and export in companies. Responses were received from all the four countries, although Ugandan customers are in dominating position compared to the others, especially Rwandan.

Testing the questionnaires prior to sending them to the elected sample ensured internal validity of the study. The testing was done so, that the questionnaires were reviewed and tested by personnel taking care of customer relations in Trade Finance, and the marketing and communications responsible in Trade and Project Finance. This ensured that the questions asked concentrated on things essential to the survey. This also ensured that the right questions with proper ingredients were asked. This increases the reliability of answers and their consistency throughout the survey questionnaires. The questions were also checked against a set of questions used in similar researches done previously (Davis 1989, Venkatesh & Davis 1996, Davis et al, 2000)

Due to the abovementioned it is concluded that the answers can be generalized to represent corporate banking – especially Trade Finance – customers in East Africa, and are valid for the purpose of this study.

3.7 Summary

Response rate of the survey reached a satisfactory level (29%). After disqualifying answers with missing data, the final response rate ended up to be 25. Majority of the sample represent thoughts of Ugandan customers; they cover almost half of the answers. Approximately 11% of the responses came from Rwanda, Kenyans and Tanzanians equally dividing the remaining part. Females were more active in answering, or simply they are majority in Trade Finance compared to males. All ages and education levels were well represented.

The validity and reliability of the answers was found to be good. This is mainly due to the variety of backgrounds among respondents and good coverage of the whole East

Africa. The sample data provides good basis for analysing the empirical results, which are represented in the following chapter.

CHAPTER FOUR

PRESENTATION AND ANALYSIS OF FINDINGS

4.0. Overview and structure of the chapter

The purpose of this chapter is to present the method for analysing the empirical results, test the hypothesis set for validating the model built in chapter 3, and evaluate the validity, reliability and generalizability of the results.

Each hypothesis is tested and analysed individually, also taking into account the background and demographics of the respondents.

4.1 Data Analysis

In total 472 customers were included in the survey, of which 137 (29 %) replied. 19 responses were disqualified due to missing answers. In total the response rate for the survey was 25%. Proportionally Kenyans were most active in answering, resulting in 47 % response rate. All of the returned answers were qualified in the research. The second best result was achieved in Uganda (35%) with the most answers qualified (55, response rate 33%). The answers received in Tanzania and Rwanda reached only somewhat over 20% response rate, resulting in less than 20 % of qualified answers (14 % and 17 %). However, the amount of individual answers included in Kenya and Tanzania was almost the same, 24 and 25 respectively. In Rwanda only 14 answers were qualified to be included in the survey.

The final sample size of the analysis is 118 out of which Rwanda covers 11,86%, Uganda 46 %, Tanzania 21 %, and Kenya 20%. 107 of the sample are users of the system, while only 11 represent non-users. From Kenya only users of the system responded to the survey, which makes the result analysing somewhat difficult for Kenyan respondents, as non-users are missing from the sample. Table 4.1 contains the response statistics per country, Figure 4.1 shows graphical representation that compares response that were valid and percentage of the respondents per country and Figure 4.1 shows graphical representation that compares total number of response that were received and the ones that were valid for inclusion in the data analysis per country

.

Table 4.1. Response statistics per country

NATION	SENT	RECEIVED	%	VALID	%
Rwanda	81	17	20.99	14	17.28
Uganda	166	58	34.94	55	33.13
Tanzania	174	38	21.84	25	14.37
Kenya	51	24	47.06	24	47.06
Total	474	137	29.03	118	25

(Primary Source, 2009)

4.2 Respondent background

The demographics taken into account in this research are gender, age and level of education. The effect of these demographics to the model and different variables are individually analysed in the results. The analysis of the respondents and their demographics are discussed in more detailed in the following sections.

Most of the answers included all demographic and background data used in this research. In Tanzania, two of the answers qualified to the research were missing education information, and in Kenya one respondent did not reveal either age or education. Rwandan and Ugandan answers included all the data demographics data requested in the questionnaire. (Table 4.2)

Table 4.2. Valid responses for the demographics

NATION	STATUS		GENDER	AGE	EDUCATION
Rwanda	N	Valid	14	14	14
Uganda	N	Valid	55	55	55
Tanzania	N	Valid	25	25	23
KENYA	N	Valid	24	23	23

N/B: - N means Number

(Primary Source, 2009)

4.2.1. Gender

Majority of the respondents were females 71% (84) and 29 % (34) males. In Uganda (44 vs. 11) and Kenya (18 vs. 6) the division is clearest, in Rwanda only slightly more females (9 vs. 5). In Tanzania both genders are most equally represented (13 vs. 12). This is most likely an indication of the division of gender in units taking care of Trade Finance in companies' in general. (Both Figure 4.1 and Table 4.3 shows gender statistics per country).

Table 4.3. Gender Statistics per country

NATION	COUNT	
	Male	Female
Rwanda	5	9
Uganda	11	44
Kenya	6	18
Tanzania	12	13

(Primary Source, 2009)

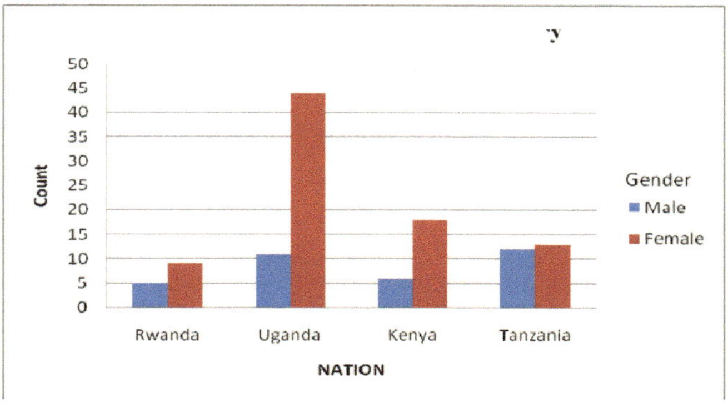

Figure 4.1. Gender Statistics per country

4.2.2. Age

The age division of the total sample is more or less expected. Youngest to answer were at age of 24, and the oldest 62 years. Average age of the respondents is approximately 42 years. Out of the sample 60% is covered with customers between 24 and 45 years of age. Proportionally the youngest respondents come from Rwanda and the oldest from Uganda and Tanzania

(Table 4.4 shows age statistics per country).

Table 4.4. Age statistics per country

NATION	COUNT			
	24-35	36-45	46-55	56-65
Rwanda	5	7	2	1
Uganda	12	17	19	7
Kenya	10	5	6	3
Tanzania	5	11	6	4

(Primary Source, 2009)

4.2.3. Education

Responses were received from customers with various education levels, from elementary/ Primary school to University Masters. 85% of the respondents have received as the highest level of education a vocational education or graduated from senior high school or polytechnic school. Only 2,5% have an elementary school level education, where as almost 29% posses a university degree. (Table 4.5)

Proportionally the respondents with highest degree of education are located in Tanzania. In other countries except Kenya all the customers had educated themselves also after elementary school. Three of the respondents did not report their education level

Table 4.5. Education statistics per country

NATION	Elementary/Primary	High School	Bachelors	Masters
Rwanda	0	3	1	2
Kenya	2	8	3	1
Uganda	0	4	9	9
Tanzania	0	12	6	5

(Primary Source, 2009)

4.3. Use of the system

Most of the responses came from users of the system (90%). Customers, who do not currently use the system, but reported that they will in the future cover 7%. Only 3% of all responses came from customers who do not use the system, and do not intend to. All Kenyan customers were users of the system, and also in Uganda only one of the responses came from a non-user. The most non-users were registered from Rwanda (36%). This can probably be explained by the distinct difference in TFIS between Rwanda and the other countries.

Table 4.6 User statistics

Usage	Frequency (%)
Don't Use and Won't	3
Don't Use but will	7
Users	90

(Primary Source, 2009)

4.4. Regression and Pearson product-moment correlation analysis

The linear regression analysis of the original model reveals that the R-square of the model is 0.128. This means the model explains 12.8% of the variance in the dependent variable, actual use of the system (table 4.7). This is not very much; meaning the fitness of the model in explaining use of the system is not high. The model is not statistically significant either, as the p-value for the model is 0.298. That is above the limit for statistical significance limit (table 4.8), which is 0.10 for weak significance and 0.05 for significance.

Table 4.7. Regression analysis summary of for the Research Model

R	R SQUARE	Adjusted R Square	Std. Error of the Estimate
0.358	0.128	0.021	0.287

(Primary Source, 2009)

Table 4.8. ANOVA for the Research model

	Sum of Squares	Df	Mean Square	F	Sig.
Regression	1.091	11	0.099	1.202	0.298

(Primary Source, 2009)

Table 4.9 contains the values for standardized coefficients of regression analysis made for the research model.

Table 4.9. Standardized Coefficients of the research model

Hypothesis	Variable	Beta	Sig.	Result
H1: Perceived Usefulness positively influences use of Trade Finance Internet Services	**PU**	0.029	0.811	Rejected
H2: Perceived Ease of Use positively influences use of Trade Finance	**PEOU_1**	0.023	0.900	Rejected
Internet Services	**PEOU_2**	0.253	0.114	Rejected
H2				
H3: Organisational Support positively influences use of Trade Finance	**OSU_1**	0.068	0.623	Rejected
Internet Services H3	**OSU_2**	-0.034	0.804	Rejected
H4: Bank Support positively influences use of Trade Finance	**BSU_1**	0.059	0.647	Rejected
Internet Services H4	**BSU_2**	0.168	0.197	Rejected

(Researcher, 2009)

As can be concluded from the table 4.9 above, according to the regression analysis, each of the hypotheses is rejected. Therefore the researcher decided to include different analysis: In addition to regression analysis, Pearson product-moment correlation analysis was conducted to each of the variables in order to examine the relationships in more detail. Each item and variable is analysed with both of the results. In addition to regression and correlation analysis, differences between ages, genders, and education levels are analysed with t-tests.

Several of the items correlated significantly with each other, suggesting that some variables influence on actual usage of the system through another variable, or in general to another independent variable. In table 4.10 Pearson product-moment correlations are shown for between each of the independent variables, and the dependent variable, use.

Table 4.10. Pearson product-moment correlations item by item

	USER	PU	PEOU_1	PEOU_2	SEF	AWE	EXP_1	EXP_2	OSU_1	OSU_2	BSU_1	BSU_2
USER	1000	0.060	0.176	0.236	-0.013	0.001	-0.104	0.094	-0.065	0.073	-0.343	0.405
PU	0.060	1,000	0.562	0.359	0.354	0.209	0.035	0.051	-0.055	-0.04	0.084	0.123
PEOU_1	0.176	0.562	1,000	0.763	0.647	0.516	0.026	0.107	-0.237	-0.172	0.096	0.153
PEOU_2	0,236	0.359	0.763	1,000	0.581	0.46	0.034	0.055	-0.271	-0.261	0.036	0.100
OSU_1	-0.065	-0.055	-0.237	-0.271	-0.262	-0.139	0.003	-0.016	1,000	0.687	0,000	-0.017
OSU_2	-0.073	-0.040	-0.172	-0.261	-0.104	-0.058	-0.061	0,000	0.687	1,000	0.085	-0.001
BSU_1	0.343	0.084	0.096	0.036	-0.014	0.033	-0.022	0.128	0,000	0.085	1,000	0.685
BSU_2	0.405	0.123	0.153	0.100	0.026	0.106	-0.065	0.101	-0.017	-0.001	0.685	1,000

(Primary Source, 2009)

As we can see from the table and figure above, 2 independent factors out of 4 prove to be significantly influencing corporate customers' use of banks Internet services. Those two are Perceived Ease of Use and Bank Support.

Each of the variables and their importance for use of the system are analysed and discussed in more detailed in the following chapters concerning hypothesis testing.

4.4.1. Test of hypothesis 1

The first hypothesis ***Perceived Usefulness positively influences use of Trade Finance Internet Services*** was based on the assumption, that the more useful the potential user experience the system or service, the more likely it is that he starts using the system. No statistically significant relationship is discovered in either regression analysis (coefficient p-value=0.811) or Pearson correlation analysis (p-value 0.525). Following the applied scale of measuring the strength of the relationship, it is less than small in this case. Hence the hypothesis 1 is not supported by the empirical results of either. The correlation figures between Perceived Usefulness and Use of the system, mean and standard deviation are presented in table 4.11.

Table 4.11. USE - PU Correlations, Mean and Standard Deviation

USE	PU
Pearson Correlation	0.06
Sig. (2-tailed)	0.525
N	113
Mean	4.26
Std. Deviation	0.874

(Primary Source, 2009)

4.4.2. Test of hypothesis 2

The second proposal, ***Perceived Ease of Use positively influences use of Trade Finance Internet Services***, suggests that the easier the customer experiences using the system, the propensity for him to use or start using the system is positively influenced. As we can see from the table 4.11, according to the Pearson product-moment correlation the empirical evidence of this study supports the second hypothesis, although regression analysis rejected it (table 4.9).

Perceived Ease of Use as a factor in trying to understand ones propensity to use TFIS is significant. There are two variables used to measure the Perceived Ease of Use. Both of them show that there is a positive correlation between PEOU and actual usage of the system. PEOU_1 Pearson product-moment correlation is 0.176, which is statistically significant

(p-value=0.06). The correlation figure for PEOU_2 is 0.236, which means the relationship is statistically significant. Judging by these results, the hypothesis 2 is supported by Pearson correlation analysis. There is a statistically significant relationship between USE and PEOU.

Table 4.12 contains the correlation figures between Perceived Ease of Use and Use of the system, together with mean and standard deviation.

Table 4.12. USE – PEOU Correlations, Mean and Standard Deviation

USE	PEOU_1	PEOU_2
Pearson Correlation	0.176	0.236
Sig. (2-tailed)	0.06	0.011
N	115	115
Mean	3.94	3.95
Std. Deviation	0.91	0.897

(Primary Source, 2009)

4.4.3. Test of hypothesis 3

Support from the users own organization was expected to positively influence use of TFIS: ***Organizational Support positively influences use of Trade Finance Internet Services.***

This hypothesis is not supported by the statistics. According to the regression and correlation analysis, both measures of this variable in the model proved to be negatively influencing the use of the Internet services for corporate banking. OSU_1 measured the importance of non-technical support and OSU_2 technical support. The correlations are almost the same (-0.065 and -0.073 respectively). Hence, it can be concluded that organisational support does not have any influence on the usage of the investigated system.

Both variables used to measure Organisational Support, and the strength of their correlation with Use is contained in table 4.15 with mean and standard deviation values.

Table 4.13. USE - OSU Correlations, Mean and Standard Deviation

USE	OSU_1	OSU_2
Pearson Correlation	-0.065	-0.73
Sig. (2-tailed)	0.497	0.44
N	113	113
Mean	2.65	2.98
Std. Deviation	1.26	1.302

(Primary Source, 2009)

4.4.4. Test of hypothesis 4

Vendor support has been studied before, and the availability of support is found to be important factor in influencing the use of Internet banking at least in Australia and Turkey (Sathye 1996 and Akinci et al. 2004) Based on this, the fifth hypothesis is ***Bank Support positively influences use of Trade Finance Internet Services.*** Although regression analysis rejected also this hypothesis, according to the Pearson correlation it is supported. The correlation is medium strong and significance is good (0.000) for both of the variables used to measure the importance of Bank Support. Hence, the sixth hypothesis is supported, and Bank Support appears to be the most important factor influencing use of corporate banking in the Internet. Pearson correlation, mean and standard deviation for Bank Support and its relationship with Use are shown in table 4.13.

Again the importance of technical and non-technical support was measured separately. Technical support correlates more with the actual usage of the systems, although the difference is not very big (0.343 and 0.405). Judging also by the results of regression analysis, availability of technical support from the bank is very important for the customers.

Table 4.14. USE - BSU Correlations, Mean and Standard Deviation

USE	BSU_1	BSU_2
Pearson Correlation	0.343	0.405
Sig. (2-tailed)	0	0
N	116	116
Mean	4.48	4.44
Std. Deviation	0.74	0.84

(Primary Source, 2009)

4.5. Adjusted research model

Due to the statistical non-significance of the research model, in order to find one that better explains corporate customers use of Internet banking services, I decided to remove some of the variables based of their standardised coefficient beta values. These values can be seen from table 4.9 above. Also the correlation analysis supports this approach (table 4.10).

The first variable removed is SEF, due to the fact that although the coefficient is the second largest (-0.250), it is also negative, which is against the assumption that all the variables would influence usage of the system positively. EXP_1 and EXP_2 are excluded due to the small values and reverse signs of the coefficients (-0.083 and

0.117). OSU_1 and OSU_2 are excluded for the same reason (0.068 and –0.034). AWE is removed due to the lowest coefficient value (0.002). PU was first excluded from the model, but the explanatory power of use suffered, and I decided to keep the variable in the model.

The Pearson product-moment correlation figures also support excluding these variables, especially Bank Support and Perceived Ease of Use, which were found statistically significant. According to coefficients (table 4.9) the biggest unique contribution to the model is made by PEOU_2 (0.253) and second biggest by BSU_2 (0.168). However, as stated before these variables were not statistically significant. None of them variables actually made statistically significant unique contribution to the regression equation (coefficient p-value > 0.05 or 0.10)

In the adjusted model, Perceived Usefulness, Perceived Ease of Use and Bank Support are measured. The R-square of the adjusted model is 0.147. This means these variables explain 14,7% of the variance of the dependent variable use, as can be seen from table 4.15. According to the ANOVA F-test the p-value= 0.005, which means the null hypothesis is rejected and this model is statistically significant (table 4.16). The variable making the biggest contribution to the model is BSU_2, which is the only one making statistically significant contribution to the use of the system in the adjusted regression equation.

Table 4.15. Regression analysis summary of the Adjusted model

R	R SQUARE	Adjusted R Square	Std. Error of the Estimate
0.384	0.147	0.106	0.329

(Primary Source, 2009)

Table 4.16. ANOVA for the Adjusted model

	Sum of Squares	Df	Mean Square	F	Sig.
Regression	1.929	5	0.386	3.562	0.005

(Primary Source, 2009)

Table 4.17 contains the values for standardized coefficients of regression analysis conducted for the adjusted research model.

Table 4.17. Standardized Coefficients of the Adjusted model

Hypothesis	Variable	Beta	Sig.	Result
H1: Perceived Usefulness positively influences use of Trade Finance Internet Services	**PU**	-0.007	0.952	Rejected
H2: Perceived Ease of Use positively influences use of Trade	**PEOU_1**	0.042	0.791	Rejected
Finance Internet Services H2	**PEOU_2**	0.115	0.417	Rejected
H4: Bank Support positively influences use of Trade Finance	**BSU_1**	0.074	0.540	Rejected
Internet Services H4	**BSU_2**	0.287	0.019	Accepted

(Primary Source, 2009)

Regression analysis for the five variables above reveals that the only hypothesis supported by the adjusted model is H4. This means, the only variable in this regression equation statistically significantly influencing use of Internet banking by corporate customers, is Bank Support. To be more specific, that is banks support in technical issues related to the system.

As Perceived Usefulness has a relatively strong mean value M=4.25, which indicates that it is a very important factor to both users and non-users of the system, I decided to study more the meaning of it. A further investigation was conducted with regression analysis, with intention to determine how the other variables correlate with PU. It was discovered that Perceived Ease of Use Explains 32.8% of the variance of Perceived Usefulness (R-square is 0.328). According the ANOVA f-test the statistical significance of this model is very strong (p-value < 0.001).

Thus, Perceived Ease of Use has an impact also on Perceived Usefulness, not only usage of a system. Although the impact of Perceived Usefulness on Use is not statistically significant, PEOU_1 has statistically significant ($p<0.001$) strong influence on PU. The standardized coefficient value for PEOU in predicting PU is 0.688. As the correlation analysis revealed, PEOU is strongly significant factor influencing usage of corporate banking services in the Internet, and now obviously also to PU.

4.6. T-tests

An independent T-test was conducted to compare the scores for each of the variables between users and non-users, females and males, older and younger, and between those with higher and lower education.

4.6.1. Differences between users and non-users

A t-test was conducted to compare the outcomes for each of the variables between users and non-users. Table 4.18 contains the outcome for this test.

Table 4.18. T-tests between users and non-users

	Mean		Levene's Test for Equality of Variances		t-test for Equality of Means
	Non-user	User	F	Sig.	Sig. (2-tailed)
PU	4.10	4.27	1.445	0.232	0.555
PEOU_1	3.56	3.97	0.197	0.658	0.185
PEOU_2	3.22	4.01	0.074	0.786	0.011
OSU_1	2.80	2.63	0.080	0.777	0.688
OSU_2	3.20	2.96	0.171	0.680	0.582
BSU_1	3.83	4.56	0.987	0.323	0.001
BSU_2	3.55	4.54	1.143	0.287	0.000

** F-value for Equal variances assumed was lower than 0.05. Therefore values for equal variances not assumed are used.*
(Primary Source, 2009)

As can be seen from the table above, both users and non-users find the system useful. Non-users seem to be more aware of using the system, and have more confidence on them when it comes to using it. Non-users also have more experience on using other bank services provided in the Internet. For non-users organisational support is more important. The only variables that are statistically significant between users and non users are PEOU_2 and BSU_1 and BSU_2 ($p < 0.05$). These three are all scored higher among the users. The finding about bank support is also in line with the regression analysis results for the adjusted model.

4.6.2. Differences between females and males

A t-test was conducted to compare the outcomes for each of the variables between females and males. The results of this comparison can be seen in table 4.19.

Table 4.19. T-tests between males and females

	Mean		Levene's Test for Equality of Variances		t-test for Equality of Means
	Female	Male	F	Sig.	Sig. (2-tailed)
PU	4.29	4.18	1.036	0.311	0.561
PEOU_1	4.10	3.53	0.896	0.346	0.002
PEOU_2	4.06	3.65	0.866	0.354	0.027
OSU_1	2.70	2.52	2.396	0.124	0.503
OSU_2	2.99	2.97	0.491	0.485	0.942
BSU_1	4.56	4.29	2.643	0.107	0.077
BSU_2	4.54	4.21	3.263	0.074	0.049

(Primary Source, 2009)

Based on the T-test results, there is statistically significant difference between the scores of males and females in Perceived Ease of Use and Bank Support. Both PEOU_1 and PEOU_2 have received higher scores by the females. Both BSU_1 and BSU_2 are statistically significant: BSU_2 somewhat more strongly (p-values<0.01 and P<0.05 respectively. Hence, females think the system is easier to use than males, but to them the importance of support received by the bank is bigger than for males – especially technical support. That is not very surprising if traditional roles and areas of interest are considered; men in general tend to be more self-assured about technical matters.

4.6.3. Differences between age groups

A t-test was conducted to compare the outcomes for each of the variables between respondents of different ages. They were divided into two categories: respondents between 24-45 years and 46-65 years. The results of this comparison can be seen in table 4.20.

Table 4.20. T-tests between Age Scales

	Mean		Levene's Test for Equality of Variances		t-test for Equality of Means
	24-45 years	**46-65 years**	**F**	**Sig.**	**Sig. (2-tailed)**
PU	4.28	4.20	0.188	0.665	0.622
PEOU_1	3.97	3.91	1.417	0.236	0.721
PEOU_2	3.94	3.98	1.270	0.262	0.843
OSU_1	2.67	2.56	0.145	0.705	0.656
OSU_2	2.94	3.00	0.436	0.510	0.819
BSU_1	4.51	4.43	0.066	0.798	0.599
BSU_2	4.60	4.18	5.181	0.025	0.009

(Primary Source, 2009)

According to the T-test between respondents of age 24-45 and 46-65, there is statistical significant difference in variables EXP_1 and BSU_2. The results indicate that the older the users are, the more experience they have in other Internet bank services and the less technical support they need from the bank. This is surprising when considering the common impression that younger are more familiar with electronic banking services, which also has been supported by empirical results in few of the studies (Akinci et al. 2004, Karjaluoto et al. 2002).

4.6.4. Differences between education levels

A t-test was conducted also for comparison of scores for each of the variables between respondents with different education levels. They were divided into two categories: respondents with elementary school, high school education, and those with university bachelor's or master's degree. Table 4.21 contains the comparison results.

Table 4.21. T-tests between Low and High educated

	Mean		Levene's Test for Equality of Variances		t-test for Equality of Means
	Lower education	**Higher education**	**F**	**Sig.**	**Sig. (2-tailed)**
PU	4.37	4.19	1.347	0.248	0.315
PEOU_1	4.00	3.96	0.938	0.335	0.806
PEOU_2	3.95	4.00	0.586	0.446	0.782
OSU_1	2.65	2.62	0.393	0.532	0.897
OSU_2	3.10	2.91	0.667	0.416	0.469
BSU_1	4.61	4.41	1.068	0.304	0.186
BSU_2	4.54	4.390	0.083	0.774	0.390

(Primary Source, 2009)

The T-test results indicate that there is a big difference in previous experience. Similarly surprising results can be seen with the education level of the respondents, as with the age and use of Internet banking of females: Clearly the higher the level of education, the less experience the respondent has with both Internet banking and other Internet services.

Again the common understanding and empirical evidence from studies done before do not support this notion.

4.6.5. Differences between nationalities

In order to distinguish the differences between Kenyan, Ugandan, Tanzanian and Rwandan respondents, a t-test was also made to compare the scores of each of the variables. The analysis of the countries and the differences of scores were done by pairing the countries for the analysis. This approach was chosen to see the differences in more detailed. Means per country are presented in table 4.22, and t-test results in table 4.23.

Table 4.22. Mean values for Kenya, Uganda, Rwanda and Tanzania

	Mean			
	RWANDA	**UGANDA**	**TANZANIA**	**KENYA**
PU	4.54	4.20	4.05	4.42
PEOU_1	4.00	3.84	3.78	4.29
PEOU_2	3.77	4.02	3.70	4.13
OSU_1	2.75	2.62	2.96	2.33
OSU_2	3.17	2.81	3.17	3.08
BSU_1	4.14	4.62	4.00	4.88
BSU_2	4.36	4.57	3.92	4.75

(Primary Source, 2009)

Table 4.23. T-tests between Kenya, Uganda, Rwanda and Tanzania

	Levene's Test for Equality of Variances and t-test for Equality of Means											
	RWANDA-UGANDA		RWANDA - KENYA		RWANDA-TANZANIA		UGANDA - KENYA		UGANDA-TANZANIA		TANZANIA - KENYA	
	F	Sig. (2-tailed)	F	Sig. (2-tailed)	F	Sig. (2-tailed)	F	Sig. (2-tailed)	F	Sig. (2-tailed)	F	Sig. (2-tailed)
PU	1.056	0.262	0.255	0.616	0.347	0.074	3.443	0.337	3.567	0.531	0.115	0.083
PEOU_1	0.102	0.558	0.863	0.341	0.269	0.494	0.521	0.039	0.097	0.810	0.143	0.054
PEOU_2	0.874	0.354	0.011	0.247	0.091	0.831	1.289	0.609	2.329	0.154	0.259	0.123
OSU_1	2.462	0.749	2.998	0.387	0.014	0.587	0.663	0.381	4.394	0.267	4.696	0.100
OSU_2	1.345	0.376	8.810	0.875	0.004	1.000	7.151	0.431	2.051	0.240	12.841	0.837
BSU_1	5.312	0.018	14.732	0.001	0.823	0.624	12.620	0.068	0.197	0.000	4.657	0.000
BSU_2	0.204	0.342	1.438	0.123	0.611	0.167	1.735	0.306	2.674	0.002	3.924	0.002

(Primary Source, 2009)

When looking at the table 4.23, several small statistically significant differences can be distinguished from the T-test results: Variable Awareness is statistically significantly lower in Uganda than in Rwanda and Kenya. Experience in other Internet services is significantly different among Rwandans and Tanzanians and Rwandans and Kenyans.

Although all the countries value support from the bank in both non-technical (BSU_1) and technical (BSU_2) issues, there is clear statistical difference between Kenyans, Ugandans and the other countries. Especially Tanzanians give the lowest scores to both: M=4.00 and M=3.92 respectively. Especially score for the technical support is significantly lower than it is for Kenyans and Ugandans. Rwandans do not see non-technical support as important as Kenyans and Ugandans either.

Tanzanians and Rwandan corporate customers obviously do not value support from the bank as much as Kenyans and Ugandan customers do. Therefore it is good to keep in mind that most of the respondents of this research were from Uganda and Kenya. However, none of the nations seem to demand much of support from their own organisations. In general, Rwandans are the least experienced, and Ugandans have the least confident and lowest level of awareness of the system usage.

4.7. Validity, reliability, generalizability

Factors negatively impacting on the validity and reliability of the results are the following:

- The fact that there are not too many non-users included in the sample. The results reflect too much the thought of the users, especially as Kenyan respondents were all current users of the system. The results would perhaps be very different if more opinions of the non-users were included, and more reliable and valid for making conclusions.
- In addition that the answers are mainly from the users, almost 46% of the responses come from Uganda. The other countries, especially Rwanda (12%) is much poorly presented. Hence, the generalisation of results to East African countries can be done, but keeping in mind that the balance of nationalities among respondents is not equal.
- Kenya, Uganda and Tanzania had the same system in use at the time of sending out the questionnaires. Rwandan customers were using stand-alone system. This

means that the system in use was otherwise similar for all the other respondents, but for Rwandans communication went only one way.

- This study is concentrated on a specific area where corporate customers do banking. However, they do reflect the thoughts of banks corporate customers' covering many industries and sizes of companies.

Generalizability of the research is or can be done for East African corporate customers of all sizes and all industries. Although the system studied in this study is an offering of one vendor, the results can be generalized to apply to similar systems. For example effect of previous experience, awareness or organizational support are clearly not important determinants for use of Internet Services by corporate customers. On the other hand, customers of other banks using the services offered by them very likely value system usefulness and the support they get from the bank a great deal.

4.8. Summary

Several different methods were used to analyse the empirical results gathered from case bank's randomly selected corporate customers using Trade Finance services. In order to find out the factors that influence corporate customers' adoption of banks' Internet services, a case of Trade Finance Internet Services was utilized. Customers from four East African countries were included: Kenya, Uganda, Rwanda and Tanzania. In the following table 4.24 the results of all the statistical analysis are summarised.

Table 4.24. Hypothesis summary

Hypothesis	Regression analysis		T-test	Pearson Product-moment correlation Analysis
	Original model	**Adjusted model**		
H1	Rejected	Rejected	Rejected	Rejected
H2	Rejected	***Supported***	***Supported***	***Supported***
H4	Rejected	***Supported***	***Supported***	***Supported***
H3	Rejected	Rejected	Rejected	Rejected

(Primary Source, 2009)

As can be seen from the table above, the original model with 7 independent variables measuring use of the system was found statistically insignificant. However, after adjusting the model based on the coefficient information from the original model and some tryouts, two hypothesis were found statistically significant: H2 – Perceived Ease of Use (PEOU) positively influences use of TFIS and H4 – Banks Support (BSU) positively influences use of TFIS. The analyses were continued with T-test analysis and Pearson product-moment correlation analysis. All of these confirmed the statistical significance of PEOU and BSU. However, no other hypothesis held for the corporate customers, which is not in line with the findings of several previous studies made.

For example the statistical insignificance of PU is against the former research findings related to TAM (Davis, 1989; Davis and Venkatesh, 19961). There is no significance of PU for the banks corporate customers when it comes to Trade Finance services provided in the Internet. Davis and Venkatesh (19961) concluded that PU has a major impact on user acceptance of a system. Sudarraj et al. (2003) validated that PU is very important factor for determining online banking usage in Canada. Chau and Lai (2004) also discovered PU to be the only major factor directly influencing the attitude towards online banking. Eriksson et al. (2004) also stated that PU is the most important factor in predicting acceptance of Internet banking among retail customers in Estonia. Only one research did notice that PEOU was more powerful predictor than PU (Wang et al, 2003), whereas most TAM-related studies have concluded that PU is the ruling factor over PEOU. In this study the regression analysis for PU revealed that PEOU is the only variable strongly influencing on PU.

Pikkarainen et al. (2004) identified PU and information of online banking significantly affecting use of online banking services in Uganda among retail customers. Neither of those, PU or OS, is supported by this research. These controversial findings are suggesting that corporate users do function in a different way compared to a situation when the system is used for private purposes.

Organisational support is insignificant to the respondents of this research. This finding is controversial to the ones made by Igbaria and Iivari (1995), Rotchanakitumnuai and Speece (2002), McFarland and Hamilton (2004) and Akinci et al. (2004). The results are very clear in this research, as the mean score for organisational support is close to or below 3 for all the nations.

Bank Support and Perceived Ease of Use are the factors that apparently most influence the use of banks Internet Services among corporate customers. Support from the banks as such has not been studied widely, but Sathye (1996) and Akinci et al. (2004) have earlier discovered the importance of information and support from the bank. It is interesting that this has not been more extensively studied, especially taking into consideration that it was the most important factor and strongest supported by the empirical results in this research.

All the studies related to TAM have examined PEOU in many ways earlier. Suh and Han (2002), Eriksson et al. (2004), Wang et al. (2003) for example have used extensions of TAM in their studies, also examining the importance of PEOU. According to them it is a key factor. However, often PEOU influences indirectly via PU. All in all, it is an important factor clearly also for corporate customers.

CHAPTER FIVE

DISCUSSIONS, CONCLUSIONS AND RECOMMENDATIONS

5.0. Overview of the chapter

This chapter is about concluding the study. It involves analysis of the contribution, managerial implications, recommendations and suggestions for further research.

5.1. Analysis of the contribution

This research was a continuum to the stream of studies related to user technology acceptance and Internet banking. The difference of this research compared to the ones made before, is the fact that the empirical part of the research was done with corporate customers. Nearly all of the studies discovered were concentrating on retail customers, which mean the private customers.

Only one research was found related to Internet banking and corporate customers (Rotchanakitumnuai and Speece 2003). That research was done in Thailand and related to the barriers of adoption of Internet banking. Several other issues and factors measured in this research were indeed studied among companies and organisations, but not in the context of online banking (McFarland and Hamilton 2004, Igbarian & Iivari 1995).

Not only has this research contributed to the area of Internet banking, user adoption and acceptance of technology and companies, it has taken into consideration four countries, an entire area geographically and economically the same, instead of a specific country as often has been the case with other companies. Another feature different from majority of the researches is that this research did not use university employees or students as the target sample. The target sample was randomly selected Trade Finance customers of the case bank in Kenya, Uganda, Rwanda and Tanzania. Although as mentioned before, this can also be seen as a limitation to the research.

The findings of this study were surprisingly controversial to those made previously. Clearly there is either difference in the way people answer about doing their own banking transactions, or when doing them in favour of the employee. Insignificance of Perceived Usefulness in all the analysis was surprising. Awareness, previous experience, self-efficacy that have been widely studied from various perspectives, did not have any meaning in this context. The results were even controversial, like previous experience in using other Internet banking services was negatively correlating with actual use – although this was not significant, it gives an idea of how much different the results were from the hypotheses set.

As suspected, Perceived Ease of Use and Bank Support were significantly influencing the use of Trade Finance Internet Services. However, it is much unexpected that the rest of the hypotheses were rejected.

Most of the findings in this research are controversial to the ones from retail side. Thus, it is reasonable to conclude that Internet bank users act in a different way depending on if they are using it for private purposes, of for the company where they work at. Naturally the nature of the case used in the study must be considered, as Trade Finance business concludes several of different issues compared to making money transfers from one account to another or buying bills.

5.2. Discussions, Suggestions, and Managerial Implications

As previously mentioned, the outcome of this study is surprising in many ways. The originally built model as such could not be validated by the empirical data. Several factors omitted from the previous researches, especially TAM, which was largely the basis for this study, failed with one of its variables in statistical significance. Although this variable, Perceived Usefulness, was finally concluded to the adjusted model with Perceived Ease of Use and Banks Support, the last was the only variable statistically supported in the regression analysis. Only the following two hypotheses were supported by the results of t-test and correlation analysis:

H2: Perceived Ease of Use positively influences use of Trade Finance Internet Services

And ***H4: Bank Support positively influences use of Trade Finance Internet Services***

Most of all it is important for the corporate customers in East Africa to have a system that can be easily used for the purpose of making banking transactions. And if there are problems while making the transactions, it is very important to have a person to contact in the bank to help in both non-technical and especially technical problems and questions. Support provided by users own organisation is irrelevant, as well as previous experience of similar services. Awareness of the things related to the system, and the empirical results of this research give a good basis for making suggestions of issues that are good for bank management to take into consideration. First of all, clearly both users and non-users think that the Internet services are worthwhile and useful in handling banking transactions. However, more variance in results could be detected among the users of the case system. This might imply that there are more expectations towards the functionalities in it. Those who already are familiar with using the service perhaps know more what is missing or additional features that would be even more useful to enhance their job performance.

It would likely be vice to take a look at the current functionality and measure it against what the customers' expectations are. Interestingly enough, Rwandan users who had the least functionality in their system, appear to be thinking the system is more useful than those of other countries, especially Tanzanians. An option to enhance the situation is to ask Tanzanian customers what are the functionalities they feel are lacking at the moment and prioritise the possible changes according to that. At the same time, Kenyan customers seem to be the happiest with the service they get online.

According to the results, elderly females do not see the system as useful as males, and younger ones. This could be because of the fact that they are not used to the system or preferring the traditional way to online work. The latter one might be more valid argument, as older females reported being among the most experienced in using other Internet services, including Internet banking. Thus, they are likely the toughest target group to whom to sell the system. Majority of the employees taking care of Trade Finance business especially in Ugandan companies are females, and most of them between 46 and 55 years old. However, at the same time the elderly are more experienced in using Internet services alike, and are the most aware of the things related to it. These results can then be suggesting that the case system is not as useful as other similar ones, or that the Trade Finance as business is more complicated and therefore complicated transactions require handling outside the system.

One of the open answer questions was related to situations when on-line customers decide not to use the system, but do the transactions outside the banks Internet service. 57% of the customers, who reported that they do so from time-to-time, claimed it is easier to do it in the traditional way, not in the Internet. Especially this was obvious in cases when there is no frequent need for this kind of transactions; the customers seem to feel it is cumbersome to get to know the system all over again every time they would need it. However, Perceived Ease of use was another very important factor of the factors in the model that was statistically significant, with medium strong relationship to usage of the system.

In general females think Internet services are easier to use. But as mentioned before, this could be due to the nature of the work females and males do in this business area: results revealed that males have more frequently upper position in the company. The same thing with users with higher education; they also were mostly men. This implies that when educating users and selling the system, different functionalities and features should be emphasized differently depending on the gender, education and position in the company.

As stated earlier, elderly women are more experienced in using Internet bank services in general. Age and gender do not have much influence on Internet experience, as well as experience as such did not have positive impact on corporate customers adopting online banking. However, it is good to keep in mind that the results imply that in other countries than Tanzania, the people with lowest level of education are the most experienced and obviously the most aware of Internet banking related things.

No matter how much experience or awareness the customers have about online banking, they all see the support provided by the bank equally important. Both items measures, non-technical and technical support from the bank was found significant. With very small difference, the younger ones especially seem to appreciate both non-technical and technical help. For all of the customers both of these are very important. The more active bank is towards the customers, the more likely it is that they will use the system and feels confident about doing it.

A surprising outcome is, that those with lowest educated do not find bank support as important as those with university degree. The lower education is, the more confident and aware the customers are. At the same time, they do not expect much support from the bank. Hence, banks marketing, selling and support strategy for the corporate customers should be planned so, that those with university degree would be provided more help and support with the system. A question is, that do they really need that support more than the others, or do they just value more the fact that support is available.

5.3. Recommendations

This study makes significant contributions to knowledge in relation to customers' perception of factors affecting Internet banking adoption. Furthermore, it also provides an insight into the customers' needs and wants which may be essential for bankers in order to provide better services to customers. In the light of these findings, several recommendations are made which may be useful for bankers and other related authorities.

Banks should make their customer more aware of their new products or services, in this, Internet banking, to encourage higher adoption rate. They can do so by having seminars, exhibitions or giving free-trial periods to allow customers to evaluate their new inventions. Besides that, education and publicity through mass media will also prove to be effective.

Banks should offer both technical and non technical support to their corporate customers as this is proved to be one of the most essential factor that influences corporate customers to adopt internet banking services.

The researcher also recommend that banks take security of their Internet banking sites into serious consideration since fraud and websites hacking still haunt most of the customers. Perhaps they can implement more advanced encryption methods and build stronger firewalls to prevent security infringement. Government authorities like Central Bank of Kenya (CBK0, Bank of Uganda (BOU) and Bank of Tanzania (BOT) can also play their role by issuing statements which reassure customer that the government recognizes Internet banking as secure.

Internet banking sites should be made as user-friendly as possible as not many consumers are familiar with computer and the Internet, especially the older and uneducated generation. Providing online help and giving customer the choice of their preferred language will ease their transactions.

If possible, banks should not charge customer for their Internet banking services. This is because users have to incur other costs. However, if this does not appear to be feasible, they would have to make sure that the costs of transacting manually does not exceed the costs of Internet banking.

Despite all the frenzy about Internet banking, bank should not neglect their branch networks. Although these branches will play fewer roles in the future, they will still be needed in selling products and services where face-to-face communication is vital. Besides that, they are the only options of cash withdrawals and deposits.

5.4. Suggestions for further research

The researcher suggestion is to conduct a research with corporate customers and Trade Finance Internet services with a larger and more versatile target group. More non-users should be involved in the study, and other corporate banking areas where different transactions are in question.

Interesting is also do individuals see Internet banking in a very different way, depending on if they are doing transactions for themselves, or for the employer. A comparison between ones thoughts regarding private Internet banking and Internet banking for work purposes as a corporate user could reveal something interesting.

In addition a wider comparison between the countries should be conducted. A deeper analysis related to the demographics and background of the users would be beneficial in order to discover how they influence corporate customers decision-making and use of Internet banking.

REFFERENCE

Africa Adventure Company,(2009), Map Of East Africa Map. Retrieved January 12, 2010) from the world wide web: www.africa-adventure.com/map/east africa

Akinci, S., Aksoy, S. & Atilgan, E. (2004), Adoption of Internet banking among sophisticated consumer segments in an advanced developing country, *The international Journal of Bank Marketing*, Vol. 22 no 3, pp. 212-232,

Bbátiz-Lazo, B. & Wood, D. (2002). *An Historical Appraisal of Information Technology in Commercial Banking, Electronic Markets*, Vol. 12, No. 3, pp.192-205, 2002

Chau, P.Y.K. & Lai, V.A.K. (2003), An Empirical Investigation of the Determinants of User Acceptance of Internet Banking, Journal of *Organizational Computing and Electronic Commerce*, Vol. 13 No. 2 pp. 123-145,

Davis, F. D., Bagozzi, R. P & Warshaw, P. R. (1989), User Acceptance of Computer Technology: a Comparison of Two Theoretical Models, Management Science, Vol. 35, No. 8,

Davis, F. D & Venkatesh. V. (1996a) A critical assessment of potential measurement Biases in the technology acceptance model: three experiments, *Int . J . Human – Computer Studies*, Vol. 45 pp. 19-45,

Davis, F. D & Venkatesh, V. (1996b) A model of the antecedents of perceived ease of use: Development and test, Decision Sciences,Vol. 27, No. 3 pp. 451-481,

Devlin, J. F. & Yeung, M. (2003), Insights into customer motivations for switching to

Internet banking, *Int. Rev. of Retail, Distribution and Consumer Research*, Vol. 13 No. 4 pp. 375–392,

Eastin, M. S.(2002), Diffusion of e-commerce: an analysis of the adoption of four e-commerce activities, *Telematics and Informatics,* Vol 19 pp. 251–267,

Epstein, Irwin, & Tripodi.T. (1977). *Research techniques for program planning, monitoring, and evaluation.* New York: Columbia University Press.

Eriksson, K., Kerem, K. & Nilsson, D. (2004), Customer acceptance of internet banking In Estonia, *International Journal of Bank Marketing,* Vol 23 No. 2 pp. 200-216.

Flavian, C. Torres, E., & Guinalíu, M. (2004), Corporate Image measurement A further problem for the tangibilization of Internet banking services, *International Journal of Bank Marketing* Vol. 22, No. 5 pp. 366-384,

Jiang, J.J., Shu, M.K. Klein, G. & Lin, B.(2000), E-commerce user behavior model: *an empirical study, Human Systems Management,* Vol. 19 pp. 265–276,

Gerrard, P. & Cunningham, J.B. (2003), The diffusion of internet banking among Singapore consumers, *International Journal of Bank Marketing,* Vol. 21, No. 1 pp. 16-28,

Goldman, A., & McDonald, S. (1987). *The group depth interview: Principles and practice.* Englewood Cliffs, NJ: Prentice-Hall.

Hernon, P. R., McClure, C. R, (1986). *Unobtrusive testing and quality of reference service.* Norwood, NJ: Ablex Publishing Corporation

Hitt, L. M., & Frei, F. X. (2002), Do Better Customers Utilize Electronic Distribution Channels? The Case of PC Banking, *Management Science*, Vol. 48, No. 6 pp. 732–748,

Igbaria, M. & Iivari, J. (1995) The Effects of Self-efficacy on Computer Usage. *Omega, Int. Mgmi Sci,* VOL.23, NO.6, 587-605.

Karjaluoto, H., Mattila, M. & Pento, T. (2002), Factors underlying attitude formation towards online banking in Finland, *International Journal of Bank Marketing* Vol. 20, No. 6 pp. 261-272,

Lassar, W. M., Manolis, C. & Lassar, S. S. (2005), The relationship between consumer Innovativeness, personal characteristics, and online banking adoption, *International Journal of Bank Marketing,* Vol 23 No. 2 pp. 176-199

Legris, P., Ingham, J. & Collerette, P. (2003) Why do people use information technology? *A critical review of the technology acceptance model, Information & Management* Vol. 40 pp. 191 -204,

Liao, Z. & Cheung, M. T. (2002), *Internet based e-banking and customer attitudes: an empirical study, Information & Management*, Vol. 39 pp. 283-295,

Liao, S., Shao, Y.P., Wang, H. & Chen. A. (1999), The adoption of virtual banking: an empirical study, *International Journal of Information Management,* Vol. 19 pp. 63-74,

Lu, H.P., Hsu, C.L . & Hsu, H.Y. (2005), *An empirical study of the effect of perceived Risk upon intention to use online applications, Information Management & Computer security,* Vol. 13 No. 2 pp. 106-120.

Lüneborg, J. L.& Nielsen, J. F. (2003), Customer-focused technology and Performance in Small and Large Banks, *European Management Journal,* Vol. 21, No.2 pp. 258-269,

McFarland, D. J. & Hamilton, D. (2004), Adding contextual specificity to the technology acceptance model, Computers in Human Behavior, *Article in Press* Vol. 39 pp. 283-295,

Morgan, R. M. & Hunt, S. D. (1994) The Commitment-Trust Theory of Relationship Marketing. *Journal of Marketing,* VOL.58, 20-38.

Pikkarainen, T., Pikkarainen, K. Karjaluoto, H. & Pahnila, S. (2004). Consumer acceptance of onlinebanking: *an extension of the technology acceptance model, Internet Research,* Vol. 14 No. 3, pp. 224–235

Rotchanakitumnuai, S. & Speece. M. (2002), Barriers to Internet Banking adoption: a qualitative study among corporate customers in Thailand, *International Journal of Bank Marketing, Vol.* 21, No. 6/7 pp. 312-323,

Sathye, M. (1999), Adoption of Internet banking by Australian consumers: an empirical investigation, *International Journal of Bank marketing*, Vol. 17 No. 7 pp. 324-334,

Shankar, V., Smith, A. K. & Rangaswamy, A. (2003), Customer satisfaction and loyalty in online and offline environments, *Intern. J. of Research in Marketing*, Vol. 20 pp. 153-175,

Shih, Y.Y & Fang, K. (2004), *The use of a decomposed theory of planned behavior to*

Study Internet banking in Taiwan, Internet Research, Vol. 14 No. 3 pp. 213–223.

Simpson, J. (2002), *The impact of the Internet in banking: observations and evidence From developed and emerging markets, Telematics and Informatics*, Vol. 19 pp. 315-330,

Sohail, A. S. & Shanmugham, B. (2003), *E-banking and customer preferences in Malaysia: An empirical investigation, Information Sciences*, Vol. 150 pp. 207-217,

Suh, B. & Han, I. (2002), *Effect of trust on customer acceptance of Internet banking, Electronic Commerce research and applications*, Vol. 1, pp. 247-263,

Sudarraj, R.P., & Wu, J. (2005), *Using information-systems constructs to study online and telephonebanking technologies, Electronic Commerce research and applications*, Article in press, 17 pages.

Szajna, B. (1996), Empirical evaluation of the Technology Acceptance Model, Management Science, Vol. 2, No. 1 pp. 85-92,

Wang, Y.S., Wang, Y-M., Lin, H-H. & Tang, T.I. (2003), Determinants of user acceptance of Internet banking: an empirical study, International Journal of Service Industry Management, Vol. 14 No. 5, pp. 501-519,

Yi, M. Y. & Hwang, Y. (2003), Predicting the use of web-based information systems: self- efficacy, enjoyment, learning goal orientation, and the technology acceptance model, *Int. J. Human- Computer Studies*, Vol. 59 pp. 431-449,

APPENDICES

Appendix A: QUESTIONNAIRE

QUESTIONNAIRE ABOUT TRADE FINANCE INTERNET SERVICES (TFIS)

The questionnaire has three (3) parts. Before each part You will find instructions for answering the questions of that part.
Please answer all questions carefully. *Note that all responses are handled anonymously!*

PART 1

Please answer the following questions by either choosing a predefined answer or writing your own answer.

1. Gender: Female ◯ Male ◯

2. Age : ___________ Years

3. Education: ◯Elementary school ◯ocational education ◯h School
   ◯ Polytechnic ◯ University
   Other____

4. Position in the company: ____________________________________

5. I handle the following Trade Finance products in general
   ◯ Import collections ◯xport collections ◯port D/C's
   ◯Export D/C's. ◯uarantees

6. ***TFIS Usage***

Are You a TFIS user? ◯es ◯ill be ◯ No, will not be

◯ No, using another banks system

a) If *Yes*, how long have You used the system? ________ Years

b) If *No, and will not be,* please specify why? ____________________________

____

____

7. If You are a TFIS user but do Trade Finance transactions also outside the system, please specify why or in which situations this happens:

◯ I am unable to access the system ◯t is easier outside the system

◯ I don't like to use the system ◯ It is easier to do in another system.

Other reasons: ____

8. If You are a TFIS user, have You ever used the available help and information sharing pages:

◯ Help ◯What's new ◯don't know what they are or where I could find them

PART 2

Please answer choosing a number that most describes what you think. The smaller number you choose the more you disagree, and the bigger the number is the more You agree with the statement. (1=totally disagree, 5=totally agree, 0=I don't know).
Please see the example below:

	Totally disagree				Totally agree	I do not know
Example						
Please circle the number closest to your answer......	*1* (circled)	*2*	*3*	*4*	*5*	*0*

Perceiced usefulness

I find / I think I would find TFIS useful in conducting Trade Finance banking transactions.. 1 2 3 4 5 0

Perceived ease of use

a) I find / I think I would find it easy to do what I want to in TFIS.. 1 2 3 4 5 0

b) I find / I think I would find TFIS easy to use...... 1 2 3 4 5 0

Self efficacy

I feel confident about using / starting to use TFIS...1 2 3 4 5 0

Awareness

I think I am well aware of issues related to using TFIS.. 1 2 3 4 5 0

Previous experience

a) I am experienced in using other Internet bank Service..1 2 3 4 5 0

b) I am experienced in using other Internet services, e.g. booking tickets, ordering goods or buying with credit card........................... 1 2 3 4 5 0

Organizational support

a) It is / would be important for me to have someone else in my organization to help out in case of *non-technical** problems with TFIS...1 2 3 4 5 0

b) It is / would be important for me to have someone else in my organization to help out in case of *technical*** problems with TFIS.........1 2 3 4 5 0

Bank support

a) It is / would be important for me to have someone to help out in the bank in case of *non-technical** problems with TFIS................... 1 2 3 4 5 0

b) It is / would be important for me to have someone to help out in the bank in case of non-*technical*** problems with TFIS.................... 1 2 3 4 5 0

** Non-Technical problem could be for example creating a template, finding a deal via Inquiry, etc)*

***Technical problem could be for example getting an error message or being logged out in the middle of a transaction*

Service

a) I think the bank is able to help me quickly in technical issues related to TFIS.. 1 2 3 4 5 0

b) I think the bank is able to help me quickly in non-technical issues related to TFIS...1 2 3 4 5 0

c) I am happy with the personal service related to TFIS I get from the bank... 1 2 3 4 5 0

Training

a) I think the bank provides sufficient training to use

TFIS.. 1 2 3 4 5 0

b) I think there are enough guides and manuals to support the use/starting to use

TFIS.. 1 2 3 4 5 0

PART 3

Please explain in your own words.

What I like about TFIS / the most valuable functions in TFIS

____

____

____

____

What I do not like about TFIS / the most useless functions in TFIS

____

____

____

____

What additional functionalities or features would be valuable for You in TFIS

____

____

____

____

Other comments:

____

MAP OF EAST AFRICA

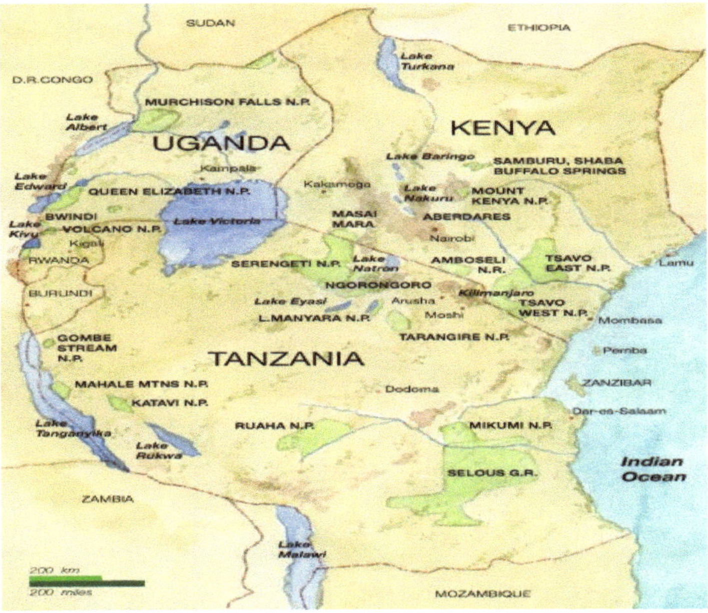

Source: www.africa-adventure.com/map/east_africa